HOW TO

GROW

MARIJUANA

The Complete Guidelines For Beginners To Grow Marijuana Indoors And Outdoors From Seed To Harvest. Product Outstanding Your Personal Or Medical Marijuana Horticulture With Step By Step Methods.

responsibility of the recipient viewers. Under no conditions will certainly any type of legal obligation or blame be held against the publisher for any sort of adjustment, damages, or monetary loss as a result of the information herein, either straight or indirectly.

Particular writers have all copyrights not held by the author.

The info here is provided for educational objectives exclusively, as well as is universal as so. The presentation of the details is without agreement or any type of kind of guarantee assurance.

The hallmarks that are made use of are without any authorization, as well as the magazine of the hallmark lacks authorization or backing by the trademark owner. All trademarks, as well as brands within this publication, are for clarifying objectives just and also are possessed by the proprietors themselves, not affiliated with this document.

Table of Contents

INTRODUCTION

Cannabis (marijuana, hashish, and hash oil) is also known as weed, pot, reefer, joint, Mary Jane, ganja, grass, sinsemilla, and dope. Additionally, blunts are cigars emptied of some tobacco and refilled with marijuana. Marijuana has been described as the most commonly used illegal drug in the United States. In 2013, there were 19.8 million current users aged 12 and older, up from 14.5 million users in 2007.30 Marijuana laws are changing and may result in an increase in use. As of January 2017, eight states (Alaska, California, Colorado, Maine, Massachusetts, Nevada, Oregon and Washington) and the District of Columbia allow the recreational use of marijuana. An additional 21 states allow for the use of medical marijuana.

Marijuana increases dopamine, which creates the euphoria or "high" associated with its use. A user may feel the urge to smoke marijuana again and again to re-create that experience. Repeated use could lead to addiction a disease where people continue to do something, even when they are aware of the severe negative conse◻uences at the personal, social, academic, and professional levels.

Cannabis may be smoked as a cigarette or in a pipe, as well as added to foods. A favorite way to use marijuana is through a "bong" in which the smoke is drawn through a layer of water that cools the smoke and removes some of the tar and irritants.

When marijuana is smoked, tetrahydrocannabinol (THC) rapidly passes from the lungs into the bloodstream, which carries the chemical to the brain and other organs throughout the body.

Contrary to common belief, marijuana is addictive. Estimates from research suggest that about 9% of users become addicted to marijuana; this number increases to 17% among those who start young. People who use marijuana may also experience a withdrawal syndrome when they stop using the drug. This withdrawal is similar to what happens to tobacco smokers when they ◻uit people report being irritable, having sleep problems, and loosing weight, which can last for several days to a few weeks after drug use is stopped. Relapse is common during this period, as

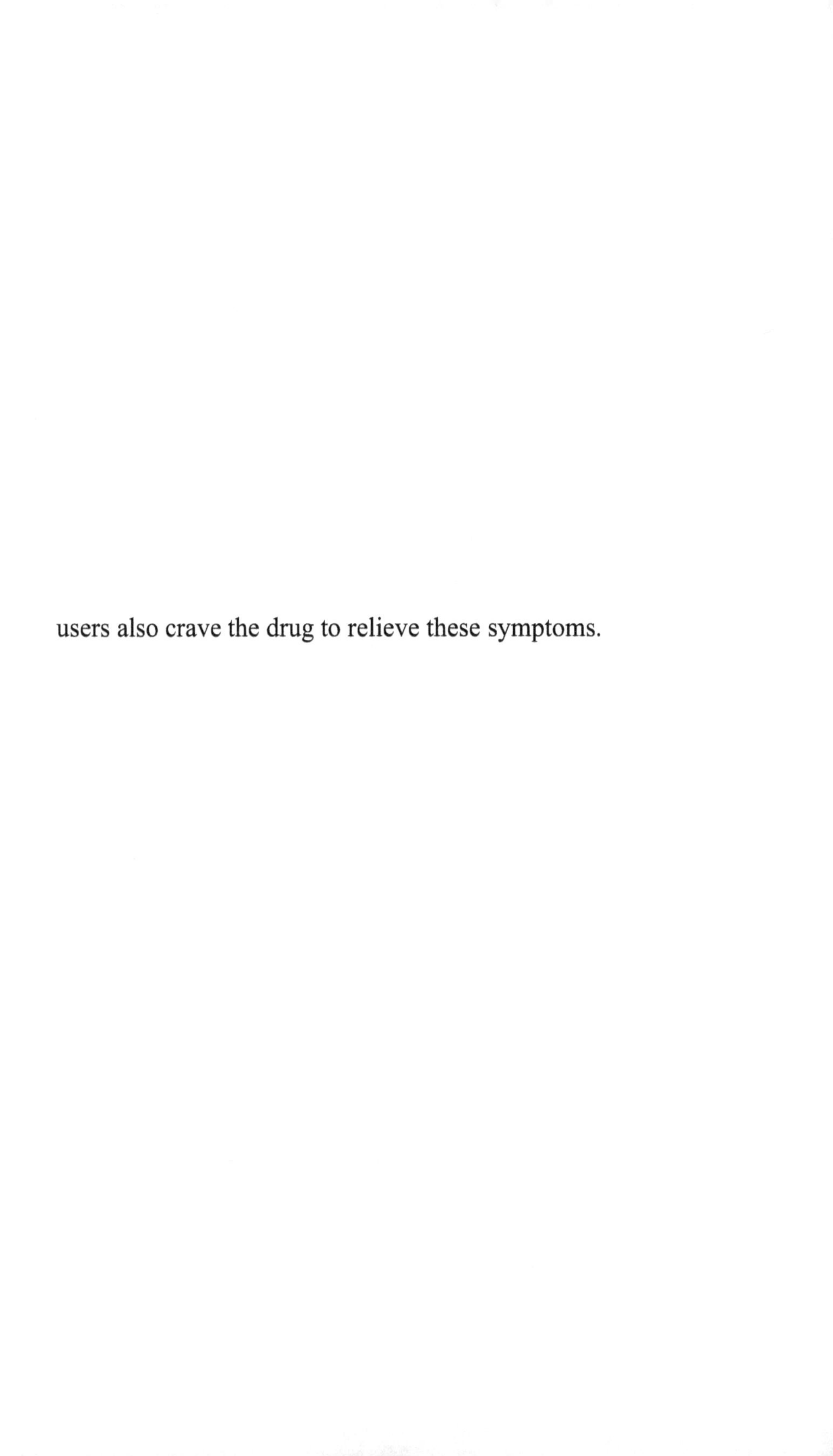

users also crave the drug to relieve these symptoms.

WHAT IS MARIJUANA?

Marijuana usually refers to the leaves that come from the cannabis plant. The main psychoactive compound in marijuana is THC, and it appears that levels of THC in marijuana are rising. Smoking THC-rich resins or extracts from cannabis, which are called by names like hash, wax, or shatter, is also increasing in popularity. There is incredible diversity among marijuana extracts, one more potent than the other. The point is that this is not the same marijuana smoked by Bill Clinton or Barack Obama.

Marijuana can be purchased relatively cheaply. In Maryland, where marijuana for recreational use remains illegal, marijuana is purchased on the street in different amounts. An ounce costs somewhere between $250 and $350, while a gram can be purchased for as little as $12 to $20. Synthetic forms of cannabis, such as K2 and Spice, which are considerably more powerful and unpredictable than marijuana and are sometimes called "parole-weed" because they do not show up on routine urinalysis testing seem to be somewhat less popular at this time.

How Is Marijuana Used?

Marijuana is usually smoked in joints, pipes, or bongs, and sometimes in little cigars, called blunts. It can also be smoked in electronic cigarettes (i.e., Juuls), making it hard to detect. An increasingly popular method of consumption is mixing it with food, known as edibles. Edible products include brownies, muffins, and candies, even lollypops. It has even become popular in certain circles to infuse challah with marijuana, though it is not clear who provides the hashgacha for this type of product.

What Are the Short-Term Effects?

Marijuana is absorbed quickly in the bloodstream and moves to the brain, causing a "high," along with an altered sense of time and a feeling of relaxation. It also tends to impair thinking, judgment, and coordination, and ordinary things often seem much funnier. Marijuana is also notorious for increasing appetite. You can tell that someone is consuming marijuana if he or she is giggling for no apparent reason and searching for potato chips. High doses of marijuana can be quite problematic, at times inducing delusions or other psychotic thinking or behavior.

Is Marijuana a Problem?

A consequence of efforts to legalize marijuana appears to be that teenagers express less concern about its negative side effects. But there seems to be plenty to worry about. Parents might consider these problems when speaking to their children about drug use.

The first problem is the possibility of developing a cannabis-use disorder. About 10 to 30% of teenagers who use marijuana report symptoms of cannabis-use disorder. The drug often interferes with everyday functioning, like doing homework or pursuing extracurricular activities. Many kids report symptoms that occur when trying to stop using the drug, such as anxiety, depression, and sleep disturbance. Among adults, about 30% of those who use marijuana report

having a disorder. As we have noted in previous articles, people with risk-factors for addiction, like a family history of addiction, cigarette smoking, untreated ADHD or mental illness, or trauma, are most prone to developing a disorder.

Second, marijuana impacts brain regions involved in executive functioning, and can lead to deficits across many cognitive domains, such as memory, problem-solving, and planning. These deficits become worse and more permanent with chronic use. There is a strong association between cannabis use and poor academic achievement. As we have noted before, doing poorly in school and feeling alienated from school culture, often has long-term negative conse□uences.

Third, marijuana users often use more of the drug than intended. Those who consume edibles, for example, are often unaware of the □uantity being consumed. Because the digestion process delays the onset of the drug's effects, people may use more marijuana than they intended. Higher doses of the drug lead to greater physical and cognitive impairment, which includes more risky decision making.

Fourth, because marijuana affects coordination, reaction time, and judgment, people smoking marijuana are more likely to get into traffic accidents. About 20% of teenagers admit that they have driven while under the influence of marijuana.

Fifth, the social nature of marijuana use increases involvement with teenagers who are using other classes of drugs. Although marijuana is unlikely a "gateway drug," it provides an obvious pathway to experimentation with other drugs of abuse.

And finally, marijuana use fre□uently co-occurs with mental health problems. Marijuana seems to worsen psychiatric symptoms like depression and anxiety and reduces the effectiveness of prescribed medications. In fact, people who smoke marijuana are much less happy and satisfied than those who do not smoke.

Therapeutic Effects

There are currently 33 states (including Maryland) that have legalized the use of marijuana for medical purposes, while 10 states have legalized recreational use for adults 21 years or older. Although medical marijuana laws vary from state to state, each state re□uires the user to have medical authorization. Research evaluating the therapeutic value of chemicals from the cannabis plant focus largely on two compounds, THC and CBD. THC seems to show potential for reducing nausea and increasing appetite, and may be helpful for reducing some types of pain. CBD, which, unlike THC, does not induce intoxication, is known to help with severe forms of epilepsy and may have other therapeutic uses, including reduction in anxiety and improving sleep. A considerable amount of research is evaluating these hypotheses.

HOW POT AFFECTS YOUR MIND AND BODY

Marijuana, weed, pot, dope, grass. They're different names for the same drug that comes from the cannabis plant. You can smoke it, vape it, drink it, or eat it. Most folks use marijuana for pleasure and recreation. But a growing number of doctors prescribe it for specific medical conditions and symptoms.

Marijuana has mind-altering compounds that affect both your brain and body. It can be addictive, and it may be harmful to some people's health. Here's what can happen when you use marijuana:

You Can Get "High"

It's why most people try pot. The main psychoactive ingredient, THC, stimulates the part of your brain that responds to pleasure, like food and sex. That unleashes a chemical called dopamine, which gives you a euphoric, relaxed feeling.

If you vape or smoke weed, the THC could get into your bloodstream quickly enough for you to get your high in seconds or minutes. The THC level usually peaks in about 30 minutes, and its effects may wear off in 1-3 hours. If you drink or eat pot, it make take many hours for you to fully sober up. You may not always know how potent your recreational marijuana might be. That also goes for most medical marijuana.

It May Affect Your Mental Health

Not everyone's experience with marijuana is pleasant. It often can leave you anxious, afraid, or panicked. Using pot may raise your chances for clinical depression or worsen the symptoms of any mental disorders you already have. Scientists aren't yet sure exactly why. In high doses, it can make you paranoid or lose touch with reality so you hear or see things that aren't there.

Your Thinking May Get Distorted

Marijuana can cloud your senses and judgment. The effects can differ depending on things like how potent your pot was, how you took it, and much marijuana you've used in the past. It might:

- ✓ Heighten your senses (colors might seem brighter and sounds might seem louder)
- ✓ Distort your sense of time
- ✓ Hurt your motor skills and make driving more dangerous
- ✓ Lower your inhibitions so you may have risky sex or take other chances

You May Get Hooked

About 1 in 10 people who use pot will become addicted. That means you can't stop using it even if it harms your relationships, job, health, or finances. The risk is greater the younger you start marijuana and the more heavily you use it. For instance, the odds of addiction are 1 in 6 if you use pot in your teens. It might be as high as 1 in 2 among those who use it every day.

You could also grow physically dependent on marijuana. Your body could go into withdrawal, leaving you irritable, restless, unable to sleep, and uninterested in eating.

It May Impair Your Brain

Marijuana can make it harder for you to focus, learn, and remember things. This seems to be a short-term effect that lasts for 24 hours or longer after you stop smoking.

But using pot heavily, especially in your teen years, may leave more permanent effects. Imaging tests with some but not all adolescents found that marijuana may physically change their brains. Specifically, they had fewer connections in parts of the brain linked to alertness, learning, and memory, and tests show lower IQ scores in some people.

Your Lungs May Hurt

Pot smoke can inflame and irritate your lungs. If you use it regularly, you could have the same breathing problems as someone who smokes cigarettes. That could mean ongoing cough with colored mucus. Your lungs may more easily pick up infections.

That's partly because THC seems to weaken some users' immune systems.

It May Ease Your Pain and Other Symptoms

Medical marijuana is legal in some form in a majority of states. And more than 10 states and Washington, DC, have legalized recreational pot. But the federal government's ban on marijuana has made it hard to study its effects on humans. Limited research shows that medicinal pot might help:

Ongoing pain (This is the most common use and a well-proven benefit of medical marijuana.)

Stiff muscles or muscle spasms from multiple sclerosis. People with MS report stronger improvements compared to measurements by experts

- ✓ Sleep problems for those with fibromyalgia, MS, and sleep apnea
- ✓ Anxiety
- ✓ Loss of appetite and weight loss in people with AIDS
- ✓ Nausea or throwing up from chemotherapy

- ✓ Seizures from epilepsy

- ✓ Dravet syndrome or Lennox-Gastaut syndrome

You May Feel Hungrier

Many people who use weed regularly notice that it boosts their appetite. They call this "the munchies." Some research suggests that might help people with AIDS, cancer, or other illnesses regain weight. Scientists are studying this and whether it's safe.

It May Harm Your Heart

Marijuana makes your heart work harder. Normally the heart beats about 50 to 70 times a minute. But that can jump to 70 to 120 beats or more per minute for 3 hours after the effects of pot kick in. The added strain plus tar and other chemicals in pot may raise your chance of heart attack or stroke. The danger is even bigger if you're older or if you already have heart problems.

It Intensifies Alcohol's Dangers

More than 1 in 10 drinkers says they have used marijuana in the past year. Combining alcohol and pot at the same time roughly doubled the odds of drunk driving or legal, professional, or personal problems compared to drinking alone.

Your Newborn Might Be Underweight

Mothers who smoke pot while pregnant face a higher risk of giving birth to underweight or premature babies. But researchers don't know enough to say if those infants are more likely to grow up to struggle in school, use drugs, or have other problems in life.

Connection to Cancer Is Unclear

Researchers haven't found any links between smoking weed and cancers in the lung, head, or the neck. Limited evidence suggests that heavy marijuana use may lead to one type of testicular cancer. We don't have enough information whether cannabis may lead to other cancers, including:

- ✓ Prostate
- ✓ Cervical
- ✓ Bladder
- ✓ Non-Hodgkin's lymphoma

WHAT'S CBD?

It's short for cannabidiol, a substance found in both marijuana and hemp plants. It doesn't make you high. CBD can be made into CBD oil and sold as pills, gels, creams, and other formulas. Some people use CBD to treat pain, seizures, and other health problems. But scientists aren't yet sure how well it works or if it's safe over the long term. Lack of regulation means you can't always know exactly what you're buying.

WAYS TO USE MARIJUANA

You can use pot in a variety of ways. Smoking usually offers the quickest way to feel its effects:

- ✓ Rolled cigarettes
- ✓ Small handheld pipes
- ✓ Water pipes, called a bong

A cigar that has been hollowed out and refilled with marijuana, called a blunt

Sticky resins drawn from the cannabis plant. Resins often are loaded with much higher amounts of THC than regular marijuana

You also can mix pot into brownies, cookies, candy, tea, and other foods. Eating and drinking the drug delay the high because it has to travel through your digestive system before the THC gets into your bloodstream. So it may take 30 minutes to 2 hours before you feel anything. But edibles give you a high that lasts much longer -- up to 8 hours -- than if you smoke or vape weed.

EFFECTS

The effects of the 120-plus cannabinoids present in cannabis are mostly unknown, but the most potent psychoactive agent identified to date is THC.

When a person smokes cannabis, THC is quickly absorbed into the bloodstream, reaching the brain within minutes.

The body absorbs THC more slowly when it is eaten, delaying the onset of action for up to 2 hours and prolonging the duration of the effect.

THC and other cannabinoids in marijuana are similar to cannabinoids produced by the body. These natural cannabinoids act like neurotransmitters that send chemical messages between nerve cells (neurons) throughout the nervous system.

These neurotransmitters affect brain areas involved in memory, thinking, concentration, movement, coordination, sensory and time perception, as well as pleasure. The receptors that respond to these cannabinoids also react to THC, which can alter and disrupt normal brain function.

Some studies have shown that THC affects areas of the brain that control memory creation and attention.

It also disrupts other parts of the brain, adversely affecting balance, posture, coordination, and reaction time. These can make it unsafe for a person using marijuana to drive a car, operate heavy machinery, or engage in sports or other potentially dangerous physical activities.

THC also stimulates specific cannabinoid receptors that increase the release of dopamine, a neurotransmitter related to feelings of pleasure.

People use marijuana to achieve a feeling of elation (a high), giddiness, and relaxation. Marijuana also produces sensory perception changes; colors may seem brighter, music more vivid, and emotions more profound. Some people experience feelings of paranoia.

When people consume cannabis for recreational purposes, they might experience the following effects:

- ✓ changes in perception, due to a slight hallucinogenic effect that can create a distorted illusion of time and space
- ✓ mood changes, leading to euphoria, feelings of energy, or a state of relaxation
- ✓ higher heart rate
- ✓ reduction in blood pressure
- ✓ impairment of concentration and memory
- ✓ reduced psychomotor coordination

- ✓ nausea, even though some cannabinoids may help reduce nausea

- ✓ increase in appetite

- ✓ faster breathing

Depending on the length and amount of use, some traces of THC might still be present in a person's urine for several months after they last used marijuana.

RISKS

Below are some examples of findings that suggest or demonstrate some of the negative conse□uences of consuming cannabis:

Impairment of judgment: A study in the BMJ found that a person is significantly more likely to crash their car if they drive within 3 hours of smoking marijuana.

Reproductive issues: According to a review of animal studies, cannabis use might lead to sexual dysfunction.

Immune response: According to one study, smoking marijuana

could eventually suppress the body's immune system, making the user more susceptible to certain types of cancer and infections.

Psychosis: Research carried out on siblings suggested that long-term marijuana use could increase the risk of developing psychosis in young adults.

Gum disease risk: One study indicated that smoking cannabis increases the risk of developing gum disease, regardless of whether the user smokes tobacco.

Reduced brain function: Researchers found that regular cannabis users who started before they were 15 years old did not score as well on brain tests as their counterparts who began using cannabis later in life.

Acute memory loss: A British study suggests that smokers of potent cannabis strains (skunk, for instance) may have a higher risk of acute memory loss.

Changes in human DNA: A British study found compelling evidence that cannabis smoke damages human DNA in such a way that the user could become more susceptible to developing cancer.

Testicular cancer: A 2015 review and meta-analysis of three earlier studies found that fre□uent or long-term marijuana use may increase the risk of developing testicular cancer, but more evidence is needed to confirm this.

ADDICTION

Marijuana may be addictive, and long-term use may cause various health problems.

Cannabis, like other pain relievers, can lead to dependence and addiction.

Over time, the severe, persistent overstimulation of the neurotransmitters that bind to cannabinoid receptors can cause changes in the brain that result in a marijuana use disorder or addiction.

According to the National Institute on Drug Abuse (NIDA), people who start using marijuana at a young age, and who are heavy users are more likely to develop a marijuana use disorder than some other users.

Cannabis withdrawal

Abrupt withdrawal from cannabis can be uncomfortable but not life-threatening.

Withdrawal begins on the second day after stopping and may persist for up to weeks.

Withdrawal symptoms include:

- ✓ anxiety
- ✓ irritability
- ✓ insomnia
- ✓ stomach pain
- ✓ decreased appetite
- ✓ Sleep problems can potentially persist beyond that time frame.

The full extent of the long-term health risks of chronic cannabis use is currently unknown. There is no way to determine who will develop severe physical, psychological, or other unwanted reactions.

Synthetic marijuana

Drugs that do not have legal status, do not have FDA approval, or both cannot be guaranteed safe.

So-called synthetic marijuana, such as K2 or Spice, is not marijuana, although it contains some of the compounds found in marijuana.

Some people may try untested and illegal synthetic cannabinoids in the belief that they are legal. This can be dangerous and possibly fatal.

Legality

Cannabis and related products, such as CBD, are legal in some states but not in others. It is important to check your state laws before purchasing marijuana, cannabis, or their derivatives.

Medical use

Researchers have been looking into the possible benefits of cannabinoids for treating different health conditions.

These include autoimmune disease, inflammation, pain, seizure disorders, psychiatric disorders and substance use disorders, withdrawal, and dependence.

CBD in medicine

Many researchers are investigating the medicinal potential of cannabidiol (CBD), a cannabinoid found in marijuana that does not have psychoactive effects.

In June 2018, following a lengthy process of research and clinical trials, the FDA approved the use of CBD to treat two rare and severe types of epilepsy that do not respond well to other treatments.

The drug is called Epidiolex, and it is a medication that derives from marijuana. It is a purified cannabidiol that does not contain THC.

Some people believe that CBD might help relieve the pain and inflammation that occurs with fibromyalgia and arthritis, for example, and possibly for treating anxiety and addiction.

THC in medication

Some studies have demonstrated that THC shows some promise for the treatment of nausea and vomiting, but its adverse effects may limit its use.

It may have antiemetic qualities that make it helpful for people undergoing chemotherapy or other treatment where nausea can be a side effect.

THC may also decrease pain, inflammation, nausea, and muscle control problems, but as yet, no medications for these conditions have approval, and more evidence is necessary to confirm their safety and effectiveness.

Some clinical trials have shown that THC has mild-to-moderate pain-relieving effects, and might be useful for the treatment of headache pain.

Studies suggest that there are specific benefits of certain types of marijuana use, and the FDA will likely approve more types of marijuana for medical applications over time.

In addition to Epidiolex, three other drugs have received FDA approval: Marinol, Syndros, and Cesamet. These medications contain synthetic substances with a similar structure to THC. They are treatment options for some kinds of anorexia.

Other researchers are looking at the potential for marijuana extracts to target and kill cancer cells, in particular as a treatment alongside radiation therapy.

Results of a study published in July 2018 found no evidence that cannabis use can reduce pain or reduce the need for opioids in pain related to cancer. However, the use of cannabis was mostly illicit and did not focus on the use of specific cannabinoids

Physical And Pharmacological Effects Of Marijuana

As a psychoactive substance, THC directly affects the central nervous system (CNS). It affects a massive range of neurotransmitters and catalyzes other biochemical and enzymatic activity as

well. The CNS is stimulated when the THC activates specific

neuroreceptors in the brain causing the various physical and emotional reactions that will be expounded on more specifically further on. The only substances that can activate neurotransmitters are substances that mimic chemicals that the brain produces naturally. The fact that THC stimulates brain function teaches scientists that the brain has natural cannabinoid receptors. It is still unclear why humans have natural cannabinoid receptors and how they work (Hazelden, 2005; Martin, 2004). What we do know is that marijuana will stimulate cannabinoid receptors up to twenty times more actively than any of the body's natural neurotransmitters ever could (Doweiko, 2009).

Perhaps the biggest mystery of all is the relationship between THC and the neurotransmitter serotonin. Serotonin receptors are among the most stimulated by all psychoactive drugs, but most specifically alcohol and nicotine. Independent of marijuana's relationship with the chemical, serotonin is already a little understood neurochemical and its supposed neuroscientific roles of functioning and purpose are still mostly hypothetical (Schuckit & Tapert, 2004). What neuroscientists have found definitively is that marijuana smokers have very high levels of serotonin activity

(Hazelden, 2005). I would hypothesize that it may be this

relationship between THC and serotonin that explains the

"marijuana maintenance program" of achieving abstinence from

alcohol and allows marijuana smokers to avoid painful withdrawal

symptoms and avoid cravings from alcohol. The efficacy of

"marijuana maintenance" for aiding alcohol abstinence is not

scientific but is a phenomenon I have personally witnessed with

numerous clients.

Interestingly, marijuana mimics so many neurological reactions of

other drugs that it is extremely difficult to classify in a specific

class. Researchers will place it in any of these categories:

psychedelic; hallucinogen; or serotonin inhibitor. It has properties

that mimic similar chemical responses as opioids. Other chemical

responses mimic stimulants (Ashton, 2001; Gold, Frost-Pineda, &

Jacobs, 2004). Hazelden (2005) classifies marijuana in its own

special class - cannabinoids. The reason for this confusion is the

complexity of the numerous psychoactive properties found within

marijuana, both known and unknown. One recent client I saw

could not recover from the visual distortions he suffered as a result of pervasive psychedelic use as long as he was still smoking marijuana. This seemed to be as a result of the psychedelic properties found within active cannabis (Ashton, 2001). Although not strong enough to produce these visual distortions on its own, marijuana was strong enough to prevent the brain from healing and recovering.

Emotions

Cannibinoid receptors are located throughout the brain thus affecting a wide variety of functioning. The most important on the emotional level is the stimulation of the brain's nucleus accumbens perverting the brain's natural reward centers. Another is that of the amygdala which controls one's emotions and fears

I have observed that the heavy marijuana smokers who I work with personally seem to share a commonality of using the drug to manage their anger. This observation has evidenced based consequences and is the basis of much scientific research. Research has in fact found that the relationship between marijuana and managing anger is clinically significant (Eftekhari, Turner,

& Larimer, 2004). Anger is a defense mechanism used to guard

against emotional consequences of adversity fueled by fear

(Cramer, 1998). As stated, fear is a primary function controlled by

the amygdala which is heavily stimulated by marijuana use

(Adolphs, Trane, Damasio, & Damaslio, 1995; Van Tuyl, 2007).

Neurophysical Effects of THC

Neurological messages between transmitters and receptors not only

control emotions and psychological functioning. It is also how the

body controls both volitional and nonvolitional functioning. The

cerebellum and the basal ganglia control all bodily movement and

coordination. These are two of the most abundantly stimulated

areas of the brain that are triggered by marijuana. This explains

marijuana's physiological effect causing altered blood pressure

(Van Tuyl, 2007), and a weakening of the muscles THC ultimately

affects all neuromotor activity to some degree

An interesting phenomena I have witnessed in almost all clients

who identify marijuana as their drug of choice is the use of marijuana smoking before eating. This is explained by effects of marijuana on the "CB-1" receptor. The CB-1 receptors in the brain are found heavily in the limbic system, or the nucleolus accumbens, which controls the reward pathways (Martin, 2004). These reward pathways are what affect the appetite and eating habits as part of the body's natural survival instinct, causing us to crave eating food and rewarding us with dopamine when we finally do (Hazeldon, 2005). Martin (2004) makes this connection, pointing out that uni□ue to marijuana users is the stimulation of the CB-1 receptor directly triggering the appetite.

What is high grade and low grade?

A current client of mine explains how he originally smoked up to fifteen joints of "low grade" marijuana daily but eventually switched to "high grade" when the low grade was starting to prove ineffective. In the end, fifteen joints of high grade marijuana were becoming ineffective for him as well. He often failed to get his "high" from that either. This entire process occurred within five years of the client's first ever experience with marijuana. What is high and low grade marijuana, and why would marijuana begin to lose its effects after a while?

The potency of marijuana is measured by the THC content within. As the market on the street becomes more competitive, the potency on the street becomes more pure. This has caused a trend in ever rising potency that responds to demand. One average joint of marijuana smoked today has the equivalent THC potency as ten average joints of marijuana smoked during the 1960's (Hazelden, 2005).

THC levels will depend mainly on what part of the cannabis leaf is being used for production. For instance cannabis buds can be between two to nine times more potent than fully developed leaves. Hash oil, a form of marijuana developed by distilling cannabis resin, can yield higher levels of THC than even high grade buds (Gold, Frost-Pineda, & Jacobs, 2004).

Tolerance

The need to raise the amount of marijuana one smokes, or the need to intensify from low grade to high grade is known clinically as tolerance. The brain is efficient. As it recognizes that neuroreceptors are being stimulated without the neurotransmitters emitting those chemical signals, the brain resourcefully lowers its chemical output so the total levels are back to normal. The smoker will not feel the high anymore as his brain is now "tolerating" the higher levels of chemicals and he or she is back to feeling normal. The smoker now raises the dose to get the old high back and the cycle continues. The smoker may find switching up in grades effective for a while. Eventually the brain can cease to produce the chemical altogether, entirely relying on the synthetic version being ingested

Why isn't there any withdrawal?

The flip side of the tolerance process is known as "dependence." As the body stops producing its own natural chemicals, it now needs the marijuana user to continue smoking in order to continue the functioning of chemicals without interruption. The body is now ordering the ingestion of the THC making it extremely difficult to quit. In fact, studies show that marijuana dependency is even more powerful than seemingly harder drugs like cocaine

With □uitting other drugs like stimulants, opioids, or alcohol the body reacts in negative and sometimes severely dangerous ways. This is due to the sudden lack of chemical input tied together with the fact that the brain has stopped its own natural neurotransmission of those chemicals long ago. This is the phenomenon of withdrawal

While research has shown comparable withdrawal reactions is marijuana users as in alcohol or other drugs (Ashton, 2001), what I have witnessed many times in my personal interaction with clients is the apparent lack of withdrawal experienced by most marijuana users. Of course they experience cravings, but they don't report having the same neurophysical withdrawal reaction that the other drug users have. Some marijuana smokers use this as their final proof that marijuana "is not a drug" and they should therefore not be subjugated to the same treatment and pursuit of recovery efforts as other drug or alcohol abusers.

The reality is that the seemingly lack of acute withdrawal is a product of the uni□ueness of how the body stores THC. While alcohol and other drugs are out of a persons system within a one to five days (Schuckit & Tapert, 2004), THC can take up to thirty days until it is fully expelled from the body (Doweiko, 2009). When THC is ingested by the smoker, it is initially distributed very rapidly through the heart, lungs, and brain (Ashton, 2001). THC however, is eventually converted into protein and becomes stored is body fat and muscle. This second process of storage in body fat reserve is a far slower process. When the user begins abstinence, fat stored THC begins its slow release back into the blood stream. While the rate of reentry into the body's system is too slow to produce any psychoactive effects, it will aid in easing the former smoker through the withdrawal process in a more manageable and pain free manner. The more one smokes the more one stores. The more body mass the smoker has, the more THC can be stored up as well (Doweiko, 2009). Thus, in very large clients I have seen it take up to thirty days before urine screens show a cleared THC level.

Similar to THC's slow taper like cleansing is the slow rate of initial onset of psychoactive response. Clients report that they do not get high smoking marijuana right away - it takes them time for their bodied to get used to it before they feel the high. This is explained by the slow absorption of THC into fatty tissue reaching peak concentrations in 4-5 days. As the THC begins to release slowly into the blood stream, the physiological response will become heightened rapidly with every new smoking of marijuana resulting in another high. As the user repeats this process and high levels of THC accumulate in the body and continue to reach the brain, the THC is finally distributed to the neocortical, limbic, sensory, and motor areas that were detailed earlier

Physiology

The neurology and neurophysiology of marijuana has been described thus far. There are many physical components of marijuana smoking as well. National Institute on Drug Abuse (2010) reports that marijuana smokers can have many of the same respiratory problems as tobacco smokers including daily cough, phlegm production, more fre□uent acute chest illness, and a heightened risk of lung infections. They □uote research showing evidence that chronic marijuana smokers, who do not smoke tobacco, have more health problems than non smokers because of respiratory illnesses.

The definitive research documenting the significant negative biophysical health effects of marijuana is not conclusive. We do know that marijuana smoke contains fifty to seventy percent more carcinogenic hydrocarbons than tobacco smoke does.

While some research shows that marijuana smokers show dysregulated growth of epithelial cells in their lung tissue which can lead to cancer, other studies have shown no positive associations at all between marijuana use and lung, upper respiratory, or upper digestive tract cancers (NIDA, 2010). Perhaps the most eye opening fact of all is that all experts agree that historically there has yet to be a single documented death reported purely as a result of marijuana smoking.

Pharmacology - "Medical Marijuana":

This last fact regarding the seemingly less harmful effects of marijuana smoking even in comparison with legal drugs like alcohol and nicotine is most often the very first □uoted by proponents of legalizing marijuana for its positive medical advantages (2007) points to the seemingly positive effects of marijuana on alzheimers, cancer, multiple sclerosis, glaucoma, and AIDS. While not scientific, personal experiences of the positive relief of sufferers from chronic illness is quoted as benefits that are claimed to outweigh the negative effects.

Including those that are legal - pose greater threats to individual health and/or society than does marijuana." She agrees that legalizing the smoking of marijuana would not justify the positive effects but posits still that the risks associated with smoking can be "mitigated by alternate routes of administration, such as vaporization" (pg. 22-23). The arguments point to clinically riskier drugs like opioids, benzodiazepines, and amphetamines that are administered by prescription on a daily basis. These drugs, like Vicodine, Xanex, or Ritalin, are internationally acceptable when deemed "medically necessary."

HOW TO GROW WEED

Looking for the basics of how to grow marijuana? Here are the tools and information on how to grow weed affordably and effectively. All you need is a small discreet space and a little bit of a budget to get started on your indoor pot production.

The first thing you'll need is a place to grow. I recommend getting yourself a decent grow tent. They're cheap, made to grow inside of and can be put up and taken down ☐uickly by one person. Some tents come with packages that include all kind of complicated hydroponic e☐uipment. Your best bet is to purchase only what you need inside the tent and to learn how to grow weed without the expensive plastic. Some even have separate chambers for vegetative growth and cloning, making them perfect for people living in one-bedroom apartments or studios with limited room to grow.

First, you'll need a growlight. I like HID (High-Intensity Discharge) lighting – HPS (High-Pressure Sodium) or MH (Metal Halide) systems with ballasts, bulbs and reflectors. If heat from these lights will be an issue, there are also LED (Light-Emitting Diode) and CFL (Compact Fluorescent) systems you can employ. Be sure to get a light that covers your tent's footprint and invest in a decent timer to control when your light turns on and off.

You'll also need an exhaust fan and activated carbon filter to reduce heat and eliminate odors. Be sure to get one that's rated for your tent's size with the proper ducting size. A clip-on circulating fan will keep air moving and stop it from being stagnant. A thermometer/hygrometer is also a must for keeping track of temperature and humidity.

If you don't have access to marijuana seeds or clones from a dispensary or friend, you'll need to get some cannabis seeds mailed to you. Don't have them mailed to the same place you plan to grow if you're not growing legally. Don't just learn how to grow weed, learn how to be discreet and not brag or bring attention to yourself.

A simple loose and airy soil mix in 3-5 gallon buckets are great for beginners and much more forgiving than any hydroponic system. Be sure to cut holes in the bottom of the buckets and use saucers under them to catch any overflow. You'll need to purchase nutrients to feed to your plants as they grow and a watering can as well.

After you've planted your seeds or rooted your clones, it's time to get them growing. Lower your reflector so that it's closer to the plants rather than making them stretch to reach for light. Raise the lighting system as your plants grow. Set your light timer to be on for 18 hours per day and off for 6 hours. During this vegetative stage, the plant will grow leaves and branches but no flowers (unless it's an auto-flowering plant).

Avoid overfeeding and overwatering your plants at all costs. Err on the side of caution as it's always easier to add more nutrients or water than it is to take them away. Marijuana roots prefer a wet/dry cycle so lift up your buckets and you'll get a better idea for if they need watering or not by the weight. The first sign of overfed plants is burnt leaf tips. The first rule of how to grow weed is to learn to stay off of its way sometimes.

Anytime space is limited for growing, some basic rules apply: Since square footage is at a premium, plans must take full advantage of each available inch. This means choosing between growing indica-dominant strains such as Hashplant, Afghani #1 or planning on using drastic trellising and training techniques if growing out sativas such as Super Silver Haze, Jack Herer or Kali Mist.

Pruning For Higher Yield

When pruning, start early and often. Cut or pinch branches just above the node where two new shoots will emerge. If you stay on top of this process, you'll have plants that look like bonsai bushes, with plenty of bud sites but not a lot of stretching out and big gaps between nodes. This is the efficient way to get bigger yields out of small spaces but your vegetating time will increase so factor that into your schedule.

Don't prune or pinch plants at all once they've begun flowering – you'll only be decreasing your harvest at that point. If the branches are threatening to reach the light, bend them or tie them down to keep them from burning. A trellis system constructed from chicken wire at canopy level (aka the ScrOG or Screen of Green system), will further spread out bud sites and increase your yields considerably. Simply train growing shoots to grow horizontally along the bottom of the screen to fill empty spots.

Flower Power

Indoors, The decision of when to induce flowering in your plants is entirely up to you. If you want to learn how to grow weed, it's important to determine how much space you have and to factor in the fact that your plants will stretch for at least a few weeks after flowering is induced. I usually recommend one week per gallon of container, so a plant in a five-gallon bucket should get approximately five weeks of vegetative time.

When you're ready to begin the flowering stage, switch your timer to a 12 hour on/12 hour off light cycle. Be sure never to interrupt the 12-hour dark period with any view. These confuse your plant and can cause serious problems.

Change your feeding regimen to one suited for flowering. Plant nutrients generally come in vegetative or flowering formulations so switch over to a "blooming" solution. Depending on the flowering time of your strain, determine when you have two weeks or so left and begin the flushing process. If you're growing a 60-day flowering strain, start to flush your grow medium with only plain water around day 46.

Harvesting, Drying and Curing

Knowing when and how to harvest your buds is as important as knowing how to grow weed.

Use a loupe or a strong magnifying scope to take a very close look at the trichomes; the tiny glandular stalk and head sometimes referred to as "crystals". Up close, they resemble little glass mushrooms with a stem that forms a bulbous round clear top. Inside that gland head resides the psychoactive compounds (THC, CBD etc). Harvest when the majority of the gland heads begin to go cloudy white and before they've gone completely amber. Harvest when they're mostly amber if you desire a more lethargic stone.

Post-harvest, you will trim and hang up your buds to dry. This process should take about a week or two depending on the humidity and heat in your area. It's always best to keep this process slower than 3-4 days in order to ensure you aren't locking in that "green" chlorophyll taste. Add a humidifier to your drying room if you think your nuggets are drying out too quickly. Never leave a fan blowing directly onto your drying colas but make sure air is circulating to avoid mold and bud-rot.

After you've determined that your buds are sufficiently dried you're ready to jar them up for the cure. The stems should snap instead of bending and the outside of the flowers should feel bone dry to the touch. The truth is there is still plenty of water stuck in the bud and the curing process will slowly "sweat" out the remaining li☐uid.

Always use opa☐ue jars (ones you can't see inside) and place them in a cool dark place. Open up the jars to determine the level of moisture and leave them open if there's any condensation forming on the inside of the glass. Slowly but surely, if you open and close the jars once or twice a day, the moist air will be replenished by dry air and the water that's stuck in the middle of your bud will work its way to the outside and then out into the air altogether. After three weeks to a month or so curing, your buds should burn and taste perfectly.

Pro Tips for Proper Drying and Curing

A key part of learning how to grow weed is mastering drying and curing techni☐ues. You do not want marijuana to dry too ☐uickly or too slowly, as the ideal drying time for a healthy and flavorful marijuana plant is 10 to 14 days. In this video, you will learn the perfect temperature and humidity to dry and cure weed, as well as pro tips that will teach you how to grow weed and trim your plants like an experienced veteran, leaving you with a grade-A product.

The Smart Pot

Attention to detail is essential if you are a beginner who is trying to learn how to grow weed. Even the most inconsequential detail could be the difference between a healthy plant and a dud. In this video, learn about the best type of container to use to grow your marijuana plant. We recommend a "smart pot," which is a container that is made of breathable fabric that allows the roots of your plant to grow much larger. Larger roots mean a larger marijuana plant, which means a more bountiful weed yield when the time comes.

The Hydroponic Garden

A hydroponic garden, also known as a "hydro" setup, is a very popular implementation to grow high-quality weed. In this video, an expert takes you through the ins and outs of a typical hydro setup, allowing you to see what it takes to successfully implement your own hydro setup at home. For those who are beginners just learning how to grow weed, a hydroponic garden may seem way too complicated to even consider. However, with some assistance from the experts at High Times, you can easily set up a hydro system that will give you an epic yield!

Pest Control and Management

As with any garden, when growing marijuana, pests are a constant concern. For anyone learning how to grow weed, it is important to become well-versed in pest management. The last thing you want is for the marijuana crop that you have been working so hard on to be eaten away by a pest infestation. This video teaches you how to ward away pests from your precious plants with integrated pest management, stopping an infestation before it can even happen. Just a few simple steps can mean the difference between victory and defeat.

Where Should I Grow Marijuana?

This is the biggest and simultaneously the simplest choice you need to make right away: should you grow marijuana indoors or outdoors? There are pros and cons to each, of course, but in the end, it comes down to what makes the most sense for your lifestyle and personal preferences as a whole.

Growing Indoors

Growing marijuana indoors can have a lot of advantages. For one thing, it's more private, so it isn't out in the open for anyone to stumble upon. It's not as expensive to set up as you might expect, and you can (and have to) control every aspect of the environment your plants are living in. If you are the type to live and let live rather than thriving in the ability to control every detail, growing indoors may not be for you.

Growing Outdoors

If you are specifically looking to save money, growing outdoors might be a better option. You won't need to purchase things such as lights (since the sun is all the light your plants will need), fans, containers for your plants or the medium they are growing in. That being said, some more unexpected surprises can come up when you're growing marijuana outdoors. Whether it's pests such as wildlife, insects, or other animals (including unwanted human visitors), privacy and security, or pollinationfrom male plants elsewhere, growing outdoors can lead to plenty of hurdles.

What kind of grow light should I use?

You should use a grow light that makes the most sense for your particular indoor setup. Although buying a grow light is specifically for indoor settings, it's still e☐ually important to think about the sun and the amount of sun exposure to your plants if they are growing outdoors. They need a minimum of eight hours of direct sunlight per day to grow the best and fastest. In general, more light leads to more (and bigger) buds at the end.

For indoor growers, you will need to choose a specific type of light. Growers use CFLs, LEDs, MH lamps, HPS lights, and more. CFLs are most commonly used by beginners since they are so inexpensive. If this is your first time, it might be a good choice. LED lights are higher in power and higher in cost (significantly) but they require less electricity than MH or CPS. The latter cost

less than LED upon purchase and highly powerful but re☐uire quite some more electricity. If you have a small grow setup, however, CFLs are likely the simplest choice for you. If you feel like splurging on the very best, go for a smaller MH/HPS grow light instead.

What kind of grow medium should I use?

The type of growing medium you choose for your marijuana plants will determine exactly how you will need to care for them. There are a lot of options besides simple soil, so it's important to do your homework and find out the pros and cons of each before choosing one.

Most beginner growers start with soilanyway, since it is the easiest option out there for the inexperienced among us. If you want to try something besides soil, you can choose between perlite, coco coir, vermiculite, and more. These are considered soilless mixes, which are a type of hydroponic growing, technically speaking. Hydroponics involves growing your marijuana plants directly in water, which can be a complicated system but a highly fruitful and rewarding one — it is said that the highest yields are achieved in hydroponics systems.

What nutrients should I feed my plants?

Unless you are using a type of soil that already includes a certain amount of nutrients, you are going to need to purchase nutrients in some form to feed to your plants. Marijuana plants need different ratios of nutrients depending on what phase of growth they are. The main types of nutrients you need to worry about are nitrogen (N), potassium (K), and phosphorus (P).

The type of nutrient "food" you purchase also depends on the growing medium you decided to use. Hydroponics systems will need nutrients mixtures made specifically for hydroponic setups, for example. This will help to maximize the growth of your marijuana plants, and will avoid causing your plants "nutrient burn."

An equally important aspect of nutrients and marijuana plants is the pH level of the soil (or other grow medium) at your plants' roots. Even the water you feed your marijuana plants needs to be pH balanced, and you should test your pH periodically and especially if your plants start exhibiting any strange symptoms. When the pH level is too acidic or alkaline, you can balance it out with a variety of methods, such as adding certain ingredients to the soil. PH imbalances can lead to plant health issues. Find more on pH levels in soil and when growing hydroponically.

Which strain of marijuana should I choose?

Now you have finally gotten to the fun part: choosing and buying the marijuana seeds to get your grow setup started.

When buying seeds, the key is to purchase them from a trusted vendor. Many Americans can buy seeds online (after checking out reviews and doing their homework as to which seeds grow best in their home climate) from vendors who ship from outside the United States. Believe it or not, no one in the United States has gone to jail just for ordering marijuana seeds from outside the US. Although shipments are always made discreetly, this can help you proceed with confidence. Choosing a strain is a completely different issue you will need to choose one that is easy for beginners to grow but also thrives in your climate. Check out the list of beginner strains below for more information.

How do I germinate marijuana seeds?

Assuming you bought seeds instead of clones, you are first going to need to germinate them. Do this by purchasing a starter cube and make sure it stays moist (not wet) and warm (not hot). Keep it this way, and you will see the beginnings of a young marijuana plant popping up after just a few days or up to a week.

If you don't have a starter cube we recommend putting them in a glass of water for a few days until they grow a little tail. This can take more than 24 hours in some cases. Make sure the temperature of the water is at 68 degrees and the PH should be around 6. When the tail is out, you can plant them.

Some people prefer to use a paper towel method instead, which involves putting seeds into a moist paper towel and within two plates to keep the moisture inside. This should take a few days to a week as well.

How do I grow marijuana plants during the vegetative stage?

The vegetative stage is when your marijuana plants are going to grow rapidly and turn into the "typical" marijuana plant that everyone recognizes. The goal of the grower is generally to get their marijuana plants to grow as fast and vigorous as possible while keeping them healthy and bushy, so they have a successful and productive flowering phase later.

An ideal temperature helps keep your plants growing strong somewhere between 70 and 85 degrees Fahrenheit should do the trick. When you're feeding your plants nutrients, be sure to feed them only half the recommended amount until the plants are growing extremely fast, and the only use three-quarters strength. During the vegetative phase, you won't know if your plants will be male or female yet which means you should ensure they are all growing quickly and efficiently. Keep the direct light on them for between 18 and 24 hours a day, or between 10 AM and 4 PM (minimum) if you are growing outdoors.

How do I grow marijuana plants during the flowering phase?

The flowering phase is the big, important stage for marijuana growers because it's when the buds finally start forming. This means that the end is near (or so it seems), and you can soon see how successful your growing season was. If you are growing indoors, you will need to change the lighting schedule to 12 hours on and 12 hours off. Keep this consistent so your plants can transition from the vegetative stage to the flowering phase and make certain that the "nighttime" part of the schedule includes completely uninterrupted darkness. If your plants are growing outdoors, they will transition naturally.

Before this point that you are going to want to remove the male plants from the bunch, or else they will pollinate the females (leading to seed production rather than bud growth). Male plants can be identified by their pollen sacs and the absence of white hairs (which will appear on maturing female plants). As soon as you can tell it's a male plant, dispose of the plant immediately.

Lower the temperature to between 65 and 80 degrees Fahrenheit for a more productive flowering phase. Be sure to monitor your plants closely, since they could experience nutrient deficiencies since they are using nutrients differently now.

How do I harvest the marijuana?

Once the buds on your marijuana plants are no longer growing white, new hairs, and at least two-thirds of the hairs have gotten darker, then harvest time is upon you. If you want to ensure that the amount of THC is maximized, you should wait until half to 70% of the hairs have darkened. If you want marijuana that leads to a highly relaxing high, wait until most (80%-90%) of the hairs have darkened.

The actual act of harvesting is incredibly easy. Just take scissors to cut off the plant's flower matter, and dispose of the rest of the plant. It's that easy!

How do I dry and cure the weed?

Once you have removed the marijuana plants' buds, the next steps

are critical. You will need to dry them out properly, without

attracting any mold. This can be pretty tricky, so tread carefully.

Hang the plant product upside down in a place that is dark and cool

and has good ventilation of some sort. Don't let them dry too

quickly.

Once they have dried out enough, you should cure them by placing

the product into mason jars that close tightly. Fill them up 75% of

the way, and leave in a dark, cool place. Open the jars once per day

for a few seconds so the moisture can be released, and some fresh air can get in. If they seem moister than they should be, you can leave off the top for longer to avoid the development of mold. Cure the marijuana product for two weeks straight, and then start opening the jars just once per week.

Many people prefer to cure their marijuana for a minimum of 30 days, but of course, it all depends on the preference of the grower—a minimum of two weeks is a good rule of thumb in any case.

Easy beginner strains

When choosing a strain to grow for your new marijuana garden, it's important to choose one that makes sense for you both as a beginner and as someone in your specific situation. You need to decide whether timing, ease of growth, yield, or potency is the most important aspect for your strain of marijuana. Let's look at some of the best strains for each option.

Fastest harvest time

The Quickest marijuana strains are usually an autoflowering strain of marijuana. These plants are consistently available to harvest between two and three months after germination. You don't have to change up the lighting with autoflowering plants, and they are most often high in CBD. Strains with higher CBD are more relaxing, making them an effective medical marijuana choice.

Keep in mind that autoflowering plants require lots of attention since the timing is so short, every moment counts. Make sure your autoflowering plant comes from a high-quality breeder.

Our fastest flowering autoflower is the Super Skunk. But with just a week longer grow time you will be a happy grower with Blueberry, Amnesia Haze, White Widow or any of our other autoflowering seeds.

Easiest to grow

For many beginners, the easiest strain to grow is the most important aspect of choosing a twist. Everything else comes in second in terms of of importance—this works well for those without a lot of extra time on their hands. These should be photoperiod strains (not auto-flowering), as it leaves more room for bouncing back in case any mistakes are made.

Northern Lights is a favorite among beginners since they don't smell very much, making it more stealthy than other strains. They don't grow too tall, making them even stealthier. They also have a high yield.

Highest yield

If you want a strain that is the easiest to get a high yield without extra, creative effort, one of the following marijuana strains is going to be the best choice.

First, let's look at Robert's very own Gold Leaf. Its buds are gigantic and heavy, and it makes for a very strong Hybrid plant and product. It can actually get to 16 ounces or more of bud on 3 s☐uare feet if grown correctly,

Northern Lights, Sour Diesel, Amnesia Haze and Super Silver Haze are among our high yielding seeds as well. Be sure to check them out!

COMMON MISTAKES

There are certain mistakes that beginners seem to make time and time again. To prevent you from making the same mistakes that countless others already have, let's look at some of them.

Ignoring pH levels

When growing marijuana, you should always keep an eye on pH

levels. This needs to be measured down near the roots of your plants since that is where they will be affected. Plants that have an unbalanced pH level will not take in nutrients as efficiently as possible. You should maintain pH the way you maintain other aspects of your grow room, including temperature and humidity.

Winging it

Whether it's not doing the proper amount of research ahead of time or it's not setting up your grow plot well enough in advance, you should never just "wing it" when it comes to growing marijuana. If you do that, all you are going to end up with is time and money wasted.

Make sure you have at least three months before harvest time because of the changing of light that comes with the seasons, this is paramount to think about. If you are growing indoors, of course, then the timing doesn't matter as much but you still need to have at least three months at your disposal, no matter the timing.

Overdoing the nutrients

One common mistake people make is feeding their marijuana

plants way too many nutrients. Although nutrients are indeed essential for your plant to perform its normal functions, more nutrients do not e□uate to faster growing.

In fact, if you overfeed your marijuana plants nutrients they could experience nutrient burn. This can lead to health issues that would have been avoided if you had underfed them instead. Try starting out with half the recommended dosage of nutrients, and then you can always increase from there (in small increments).

Overwatering

Along with overdosing your plants on nutrients, overwatering your plants can lead to a number of issues as well. This is most common with beginners because they want to make sure their plants always have enough water but in the end, soil that is constantly wet is more prone to things like mold and mildew, or even drowning the plant (depriving its roots of enough oxygen).

It is easier to make up for underwatering than overwatering, so make sure that an inch or so of the soil is dry before you water again.

Skimping on costs

There are a certain amount of costs that can be saved safely when growing marijuana plants, but that does not mean that you should skimp on prices everywhere. For example, buying cheap seeds is not a good way to save money in fact, it's a good way to waste money.

Growing outdoors, however, can be an effective way to cut costs, or else to opt for a soil grow setup rather than a hydroponics one. Buying certain things secondhand (such as light fixtures, fans, and so on) can also help reduce costs without lowering the quality of your setup

MARIJUANA ADDICTION SYMPTOMS TREATMENT

Marijuana, cannabis, chronic, dope, ganja, grass, mary jane, pot or whatever people may call it, is a non-synthetic substance that comes from the plant cannabis sativa and cannabis indica. Its colors and characteristics vary depending where it is grown but its common hue is green. In the late 1800s the use and sale of Marijuana were regulated by a number of states and local governments in America. In 1906, several states controlled the drug by labeling it as a poison. By the 1920s, prohibition of the drug was entered in the constitution, and it was then repealed in the 1930s. Ever since, marijuana use continued to be illegal in the United States.

The marijuana plant is intended as a psychoactive drug. Our ancestors use them as a recreational drug and they use it for religious rituals as well. The use of marijuana is comparable to any other addictions such as alcohol abuse, cigarette, heroin and other drug exploitations. They have negative effects on man's health.

Common side effects includes memory loss, slow learning, lack of concentration, loss of coordination, paranoia, emotional instabilities, poor perception or judgment.

Many people who are addicted to marijuana are hooked to its psychoactive effects due to the substance called THC or delta-9-tetrahydrocannabinol, which is the primary active component of marijuana. This substance is known to have a stimulant, depressant or hallucinogen effect. THC allows the brain to release its dopamine, a substance commonly known as pleasure chemical, giving the user a euphoric high. Euphoric sense is the main reason why people are getting hooked-up with marijuana.

Marijuana addiction is considered as a disease in many societies. Several groups considered marijuana users as outcasts. Thus, it lowers their confidence and morale towards self. Symptoms of addiction are loss of control over the drug and helplessness to quit regardless of the efforts exerted. Alongside with these symptoms, a strong urge of smoking marijuana is very common to the marijuana addicts. Whenever they failed to smoke, they feel depressed, anxious, unable to focus on other things and easily get angered.

According to research, treating marijuana addiction is not easy. Experts believe that there are no distinct medication to treat this kind of addiction. Treatment is the combination of detoxification, awareness on the bad effects of marijuana to the body, support of friends, families and loved-ones.

Detoxification - Experts believe that detoxification is the key therapy to treat chronic users of marijuana. Detoxification usually includes healthy diet, regular exercise, increase water intake and for some, detox pills. The detox program is directed at the physical effects of marijuana. Rehabilitation on the other hand, is a long-range goal so that the abuser will be completely free of the substance. The target of the program is lifestyle modifications.

Awareness - Many users are unaware of the bad effects of the marijuana to their physical, psychological and social being. Gaining knowledge on the harmful effects of marijuana can help chronic users to abstain from marijuana.

Moral support - As mentioned earlier, one reason why chronic users are having difficulty of quitting the drug and why relapses occur, is the lack of support from the people that surround them. Users need understanding, love, patience and special attention. Understanding will greatly help them in quitting the drug.

Marijuana addiction truly affects many people in different walks of life. Though marijuana use is illegal in the United States, it continues to be the most abused illicit drug in the most powerful country in the world. Aside from America, marijuana has been banned in many countries because of its various negative effects on man. In spite the prohibition, the abusers continue to grow. It is significant not to eliminate the importance of information dissemination about marijuana and other drugs so that people will not have to use it out of curiosity

Is Marijuana Good For Your Health?

Yes marijuana is good for your health. Medical marijuana that is. Today there is increasing interest in the use of medical marijuana for treating everything from cancer to menstrual cramps and migraine headaches. People who wouldn't be caught dead using marijuana are now interested in medical marijuana because it may

be able to save their lives.

Medical professionals worldwide have used marijuana for

millennia to treat a variety of ailments. Modern medicine men are

begrudgingly beginning to acknowledge medical marijuana can aid

in the treatment and cure of many diseases.

Earliest Usage

Marijuana, or more properly Cannabis Sativa, has been used for its

medicinal properties for over 5,000 years. Its earliest documented

use is in China. In the 28th Century B.C. the Chinese Emperor

Shen-Nung prescribed marijuana for gout, beriberi, constipation,

'female weakness', rheumatism and malaria among other ailments.

In 2,000 B.C. physicians in Egypt were prescribing marijuana for

eye problems. In India in 1,000 B.C. marijuana was being used as

an anesthetic and an anti-phlegmatic and Hoa-Tho, a 2nd Century

A.D. Chinese physician is reported to have used marijuana as an

analgesic during surgery.

Modern Usage

Today in many parts of India and especially in Ayer Vedic medicine marijuana is used to treat a wide range of ailments. It is also used as a sedative, an analgesic, an anti-hemorrhoidal and an antispasmodic.

One might infer marijuana is only used in 'backward' Asian countries with no knowledge of modern medical practices, But one would be wrong. Napoleon's army used it to treat burns, as a sedative and as a pain reliever. In the United States in 1961 the National Institute of Mental Health did a study that indicated marijuana could be used for epilepsy, infant convulsions, treatment of tetanus, convulsions of rabies, treatment of depression, as a sedative and hypnotic in relieving anxiety and has antibiotic properties.

Today physicians prescribe medicinal marijuana to stimulate the appetite of AIDS patients, treat glaucoma and multiple sclerosis and reduce nausea for cancer patients. The British House of Lords in a 2001 report stated marijuana could be used to treat migraine headaches, schizophrenia, asthma, arthritis, multiple sclerosis and general pain. Doctors also acknowledge it can help to treat high blood pressure.

Medical Marijuana Movement

There is a major movement, particularly in California, to make medicinal marijuana readily available to patients through medicinal marijuana stores. California medicinal marijuana dispensaries and medicinal marijuana clinics, many of which are run by medicinal marijuana collectives and marijuana doctors, seek to make medicinal marijuana available to patients with medical weed cards that legally allow them to receive medical marijuana strains to treat a variety of illnesses. Medical marijuana is truly becoming a herb for the healing of the nation.

Marijuana Withdrawal Symptoms

Is marijuana addictive? Does marijuana cause health problems? The answers to those ☐uestions have been the subject of many debates and arguments over the years. However, there is research that has proven that marijuana can indeed be addictive and it does pose health problems. But, even with the evidence from research, the subject is still highly controversial.

Although not everyone that uses marijuana will become addicted, some people will. It's estimated that approximately 9% of the people that use marijuana do become physically dependent. That number rises to around 1 in 6 for those who started using marijuana at a young age. And, for those who use marijuana on a daily basis, that number rises to as much as half.

One study included almost 500 heavy marijuana users that were trying to quit. Of that number, around one-third started using marijuana again to relieve the withdrawal symptoms. Over 42% reported experiencing at least one of the symptoms of marijuana withdrawal. And, other studies have had similar results.

Habitual marijuana users can expect to start experiencing marijuana withdrawal symptoms within around 8 hours after the last use. The symptoms are more prominent during the first 10 days. However, most symptoms start to subside within the first 3 to 4 days. The full process of marijuana withdrawal can last for up to 45 days.

The most common marijuana withdrawal symptom is anxiety. It's one of the biggest problems especially during the first few weeks of withdrawal. While the anxiety levels are generally mild to moderate, it is constant. Many people experience drastic mood changes and behave differently. Aggression is often increased and the person may get angry much faster than normal.

Many of the symptoms of marijuana withdrawal are opposites of the effects of using marijuana. Instead of feeling hungry, or having the "munchies" most people lose their appetite and barely eat anything. Instead of feeling drowsy, some people find it difficult to sleep at all. Instead of feeling relaxed, most people become restless.

Generally a loss of appetite will only last for several days after the last use of marijuana. Some people will feel constantly nauseated and some have diarrhea. Insomnia is at it's worst during the first few days, but it's not uncommon to have difficulty sleeping for weeks. However, sleep patterns will return to normal.

Marijuana use causes an interference in a mechanism of consciousness that causes you to dream. In most cases, the person either doesn't dream or can't remember their dreams. When the person stops using marijuana, dreams return when they can sleep. Nightmares are very common and they seem to be very real and vivid.

Although marijuana is certainly not the most dangerous drug, it does pose some health problems. Marijuana contains over 400 different chemicals. Just one marijuana cigarette has almost four times as much tar as a regular cigarette. During the first hour after someone has smoked marijuana the risk of them having a heart attack is increased five times. Among other things it weakens the immune system, increases a persons risk of developing lung infections

MEDICAL MARIJUANA: IT REALLY IS A HEALING HERB

Medical Marijuana has been used for healing for thousands of years. In ancient China, India, the Middle East and even America the herb had been identified as having medicinal properties. Even in more modern times Queen Victoria and her personal physician did some groundbreaking work into the medical application of marijuana. The herb had also been in common use in the United States prior to the passing of the Stamp Act in the 1920s and other marijuana laws. Today patients suffering with asthma, A.I.D.S, cancer and many other illnesses extol the virtues of marijuana use.

The History

Marijuana, or Cannabis Sativa as it is known scientifically, is an herb that grows wild in temperate climates. Long before teenagers and counter culture activists were experimenting with cannabis many Asian countries had long since included medicinal marijuana on their list of healing herbs. The earliest documented use of this medicinal weed is among the Chinese. The therapeutic use of medicinal marijuana was documented by Emperor Shen-Nuan in the 28th century B.C. He wrote of its value for treating malaria, constipation, rheumatism, gout and other maladies.

How Is It Used?

Medical weed can be used in a variety of ways. Some medicinal marijuana physicians prepare it as a liquid for drinking. Other health professionals feel pot is more effective when it is eaten. Smoking is another means of getting the healing properties of medical pot into the body of the person who needs healing. Some marijuana doctors crush the weed and use it as an ointment or in a poultice.

Today California is ground Zero in the battle for marijuana legalization. Since the passage of Prop 215 California residents have set up a series of medicinal marijuana shops. There are also a number of marijuana vending machines in several locations throughout the state. With a California medicinal marijuana card or a cannabis club card California residents can legally obtain medical marijuana from any of the medical marijuana dispensaries in the state. To obtain a card Californians must receive a marijuana evaluation by one of the medical marijuana doctors in the state.

Opening a medical marijuana dispensary is not very difficult in California. This has led to a string medical marijuana evaluation centers where California medical marijuana licenses can be issued. While decriminalization of medical marijuana has been an important step many marijuana activists have vowed to stop at nothing short of making weed legal in California. Large segments of the population are pro medical marijuana. This has made members of the marijuana legalization movement confident they will eventually be successful.

EFFECTS OF MARIJUANA ON YOUR BODY

Marijuana is made from the shredded and dried parts of the cannabis plant, including the flowers, seeds, leaves, and stems. It's also known as pot, weed, hash, and dozens of other names. While many people smoke or vape it, you can also consume marijuana as an ingredient in food, brewed tea, or oils.

Different methods of taking the drug may affect your body differently. When you inhale marijuana smoke into your lungs, the drug is □uickly released into your bloodstream and makes its way to your brain and other organs. It takes a little longer to feel the effects if you eat or drink marijuana.

There is ongoing controversy around the effects of marijuana on the body. People report various physical and psychological effects, from harm and discomfort to pain relief and relaxation.

Here's what happens to your body when this drug enters your bloodstream.

Marijuana can be used in some states for medical reasons, and in some areas, recreational use is legal as well. No matter how you use marijuana, the drug can cause immediate and long-term effects, such as changes in perception and increased heart rate. Over time, smoking marijuana may cause chronic cough and other health issues.

The effects of marijuana on the body are often immediate. Longer-term effects may depend on how you take it, how much you use, and how often you use it. The exact effects are hard to determine because marijuana has been illegal in the U.S., making studies difficult and expensive to conduct.

But in recent years, the medicinal properties of marijuana are gaining public acceptance. As of 2017, 29 states plus the District of Columbia have legalized medical marijuana to some extent. THC and another ingredient called cannabidiol (CBD) are the main substances of therapeutic interest. The National Institutes of Health funded research into the possible medicinal uses of THC and CBD, which is still ongoing.

With the potential for increased recreational use, knowing the effects that marijuana can have on your body is as important as ever. Read on to see how it affects each system in your body.

Respiratory system

Much like tobacco smoke, marijuana smoke is made up of a variety of toxic chemicals, including ammonia and hydrogen cyanide, which can irritate your bronchial passages and lungs. If you're a regular smoker, you're more likely to wheeze, cough, and produce phlegm. You're also at an increased risk of bronchitis and lung infections. Marijuana may aggravate existing respiratory illnesses, such as asthma and cystic fibrosis.

Marijuana smoke contains carcinogens, so it may increase your risk of lung cancer too. However, studies on the subject have had mixed results. According to the National Institute of Drug Abuse (NIDA), there is no conclusive evidence that marijuana smoke causes lung cancer. More research is needed.

Circulatory system

THC moves from your lungs into your bloodstream and throughout your body. Within minutes, your heart rate may increase by 20 to

50 beats per minute. That rapid heartbeat can continue for up to three hours. If you have heart disease, this could raise your risk of heart attack.

One of the telltale signs of recent marijuana use is bloodshot eyes. The eyes look red because marijuana causes blood vessels in the eyes to expand.

THC can also lower pressure in the eyes, which can ease symptoms of glaucoma for a few hours. More research is needed to understand the active ingredients in marijuana and whether it's a good treatment for glaucoma.

In the long term, marijuana has a possible positive effect on your circulatory system. isn't conclusive yet, but marijuana may help stop the growth of blood vessels that feed cancerous tumors. Opportunities exist in both cancer treatment and prevention, but more research is needed.

Central nervous system

The effects of marijuana extend throughout the central nervous system (CNS). Marijuana is thought to ease pain and inflammation and help control spasms and seizures. Still, there are some long-term negative effects on the CNS to consider.

THC triggers your brain to release large amounts of dopamine, a naturally occurring "feel good" chemical. It's what gives you a pleasant high. It may heighten your sensory perception and your perception of time. In the hippocampus, THC changes the way you process information, so your judgment may be impaired. The hippocampus is responsible for memory, so it may also be difficult to form new memories when you're high.

Changes also take place in the cerebellum and basal ganglia, brain areas that play roles in movement and balance. Marijuana may alter your balance, coordination, and reflex response. All those changes mean that it's not safe to drive.

Very large doses of marijuana or high concentrations of THC can cause hallucinations or delusions. According to the NIDA, there may be an association between marijuana use and some mental health disorders like depression and anxiety. More research is needed to understand the connection. You may want to avoid marijuana if you have schizophrenia, as it may make symptoms worse.

When you come down from the high, you may feel tired or a bit depressed. In some people, marijuana can cause anxiety. About 30 percent of of marijuana users develop a pot use disorder. Addiction is considered rare but very real. Symptoms of withdrawal may includes irritability, insomnia, and loss of appetite.

In people younger than 25 years, whose brains have not yet fully developed, marijuana can have a lasting impact on thinking and memory processes. Using marijuana while pregnant can also affect the mind of your unborn baby. Your child may have trouble with memory, concentration, and problem-solving skills.

Digestive system

Smoking marijuana can cause some stinging or burning in your mouth and throat while you're inhaling.

Marijuana can cause digestive issues when taken orally. For example, oral THC can cause nausea and vomiting because of the way it's processed in your liver. It may also damage your liver.

Conversely, marijuana has also been used to ease symptoms of nausea or upset stomach.

An increase in your appetite is common when taking any form of marijuana, leading to what many call "the munchies." This is considered a benefit for people being treated with chemotherapy for cancer. For others who are looking to lose weight, this effect could be considered a disadvantage.

Immune system

THC may adversely affect your immune system. StudiesTrusted Source involving animals showed that THC might damage the immune system, making you more vulnerable to illnesses. Further research is needed to fully understand the effects.

WHY YOU SHOULD CONSIDER QUITTING MARIJUANA

There are a million reasons why people should not smoke marijuana. For starters, marijuana contains delta-9-tetrahydrocannabinol, better known as THC but it also contains in excess of 400 additional chemicals too. The marijuana of the 2000's is much more potent than the marijuana that was smoked back 30 or 40 years ago.

This newer strain of marijuana causes people's heart and pulse to race, it impairs memory, hinders concentration, and it thwarts coordination and reaction time. In some people marijuana causes anxiety and panic. It is also proven to be psychologically dependent. Those who smoke marijuana develop a tolerance and need more to get the same effect as they once did.

For young people, marijuana is even worse.

Most teens who smoke marijuana lose interest in school and extracurricular activities. This may have a lot to do with the fact that marijuana damages the brain and hinders things such as thinking and comprehension. Teens also have a tendency to experiment further and use other drugs when they start young.

Since marijuana slows reaction times down it is not advised to smoke and drive. Marijuana also tampers with the reproductive system. It causes babies to be premature when the mother smokes it during pregnancy and it causes lower fertility rates in both men and women. In addition, marijuana does damage to both the heart and the lungs.

Marijuana increases the heart rate by up to 50% which can be dangerous. Because marijuana smoke is unfiltered, breathed in deeply and then held in it is more dangerous than cigarettes. Marijuana and its carcinogens can cause cancer. The threat is just as real as it is for smoking cigarettes.

Another problem with marijuana is that it sticks around for a very long time, even after the buzz is gone. Most illicit drugs are out of a person's system within three days but not marijuana which can hang around for as long as 45 days. THC stores itself in a person's fat tissues.

It is the natural job of the body to try to remove these chemicals so it converts them into metabolites. This is precisely why it takes so long to be able to test clean for marijuana on a urine test.

Marijuana has an impact on the central nervous system that will attach to the brain's neurons and plays havoc on their ability to communicate with each other. It is these neurons that are responsible for short-term memory, for example. Out of all the chemicals found in marijuana, THC is the most problematic.

THC actually binds to the cannabinoid receptors and alters coordination, the thought process, and concentration. And that's not all.

THC upsets the production of different neurotransmitters, which act as messengers in the brain. This can cause the onset of depression, personality disorders, and anxiety. Marijuana also damages a person's emotions. This is brought about by the euphoric feelings that marijuana causes and why many people who smoke it display a carefree attitude while they are high.

There are countless reasons why a person should quit smoking marijuana. Marijuana causes people to feel sluggish, unmotivated, and often even lazy. People refer to this as feeling "burned out" and it is a syndrome that is all too well-known amongst pot smokers. The feeling of not having any motivation is enough reason for many smokers to stop.

A final thought to keep in mind is that smoking just one marijuana cigarette is the same as smoking between 2.5 and five cigarettes, depending on the potency. This means that it is certain that marijuana smoke can and likely will cause some type of respiratory problems.

Quitting marijuana can be a scary endeavor for some people and even for those who have tried to stop and have failed it is essential to know that help is available. Quitting is an option and it can be done successfully.

Why Chronic Marijuana Smokers Can't Quit

Countless everyday people begin smoking cannabis as teenagers. On the other hand, it's not unusual to discover individuals who start a cannabis dependency way into their adult years. Regardless of what age range in which you were introduced to cannabis, it occurs in a similar way for most of us: influence from friends or sometimes family. Lots of people truly don't prefer the feeling pot produces at first however after a couple of more attempts they may begin to crave it. What started out as experimentation builds up to an ongoing exercise. This kind of frequent use of a drug where someone cannot go very long without it in order to feel good is in many instances called self-medicating.

Generally people don't even know when they are self-medicating. Each person has their own particular reasons to regularly use marijuana but no matter if we acknowledge it or not, it's a method of lessening the demands associated with everyday living. After a difficult business day for example, dependent weed users can barely hold on until the moment they breathe a huge cloud of cannabis smoke into their respiratory system to really feel optimal yet again.

If you can associate with what I'm expressing here in any respect, you may be at an important juncture, where you can fully grasp that blazing up repeatedly to alleviate the demands of living sooner or later results in an enormous cloud over your head (pun intended).

A Marijuana Smoker's Primary Rationalizations to Continue Smoking Pot

Below are just a few of the many rationalizations coming from individuals that keep up their marijuana routine. Can you connect with any of these? If not, in all probability you don't have a significant marijuana dependency. Please know there's absolutely no motive to be judge anyone. I WAS a long-term bud fanatic too.

"Marijuana minimizes my symptoms of depression"

I made use of this particular justification too but I started to figure out that although it granted me short-term alleviation, pot use amplified my depressive tendencies over time. A typical attribute of any substance dependency is that the conduct designed to lessen unwanted emotions and thoughts simply worsens the worries we're trying to steer clear of. Thus we engage in an endless routine of medicating our own unhappiness while extending it at the same time.

"The people I most closely associate with smoke weed"

Many people get started using marijuana to acuire "interesting" people to hang with. However, the eventual outcome for the majority of enthusiastic pot smokers is they start smoking by themselves more regularly than they do with other people resulting in a gradual withdrawal from society. In any case, grass might be trendy to other people who smoke but it's not so awesome to individuals who are really doing something in life.

"Smoking weed is just plain enjoyable"

Yes, it can be enjoyable. Nevertheless, the economic, psychological, legal, and other ramifications of marijuana smoking are not as enjoyable.

"Smoking marijuana is good for you"

Incredibly enough, numerous smokers will argue that marijuana use is healthful in that it reduces the daily strains on the human body. This particular reason may possibly endure if the marijuana is smoked □uite moderately, Some folks may be have the power to light up infre□uently, most users don't have this ability. Constant marijuana smoking has considerably more damaging effects on wellness compared to the positive.

"Legalization seems to be a foregone conclusion, so then I won't have to worry about getting in trouble with legal authorities"

Legalization of marijuana is an emerging trend. Alcoholic beverages have been allowed by the law for a quite a while in most countries too but this isn't a great reason to turn into a drunk. We are not targeting the merits of legalization here. We're going over the underlying complications and unfavorable outcomes of prolonged marijuana smoking.

"Weed Smoking gets me extremely focused"

This is another popular rationalization. I would fire up and get particularly zoned into a particular undertaking and be □uite effective for a short time. Nonetheless, poor attention would at some point take over, I would light up again and after that get nothing else accomplished.

"Marijuana bolsters innovation"

We unquestionably think at an exceptionally innovative degree whenever stoned. There are countless performing artists of all types who proclaim the creative attributes of cannabis on what they do. Nevertheless, I challenge you to name anyone who has a prolonged marijuana reliance while still managing an all encompassing success in life.

"Marijuana enables me to sleep"

Okay, it does tends to assist you to fall asleep, but there have been a number of clinical studies that indicate THC hinders the natural cycles of sleep therefore blocking the deep sleep a body re uires. This is probably the reason why a number of chronic weed smokers need to smoke first thing in the morning; it helps reduce the discomfort associated with not having a good sleep.

"Marijuana elevates metaphysical awareness"

Many individuals experience intense, original thought processes whenever smoking marijuana. This is especially true during the early phases of establishing a dependence. Many of us blaze up and discover ourselves speaking directly to the Great Spirit, caring for our friends a good deal more, and so on. What I've learned though is it is merely an artificial way to experiencing the divine. If spirituality is what you seek out, find people who have a rewarding spiritual way of life without marijuana. You might be shocked at what you find out.

" Marijuana intensifies all my activities"

I believe this is the challenge which helps to keep the addiction going for a great many marijuana smokers. When we're high, meals are more delicious, songs sounds more amazing, other people become more appealing, and the list goes on. I think this is the most difficult component of getting stoned to conquer because it seems to just make life less drab. I ultimately came to the realization that despite the fact that marijuana does deliver experiences of joy here and there, it steals away any perpetual satisfaction with one's life.

There is something I deliberately held off the list as a rationalization: medical marijuana. A professionally identified wellness issue is a respectable purpose for a marijuana smoking routine. One should adhere to their physician's guidance if he or she recommended medical marijuana.

MARIJUANA, THE MYTHS AND FACTS

A drug, Marijuana, prepared for human consumption in an herbal form is also called by Cannabis, one among its several names. Everyone should be apprised of the fact that using Marijuana is in fact Drug abuse. People have termed Marijuana safer to use than other drugs and tried to whitewash it; however, real psychological harm and physical harm are caused. The fact is that Marijuana is a hallucinogenic drug, that can lead to addiction and abuse.

Symptoms Of Marijuana's Addiction

Both emotional and mental addictions are caused by Marijuana. The mind becomes Marijuana obsessed and you start gravitating towards friends and people who are like minded. Once the addiction is full blown the person is only able to function under the Marijuana high. Their misconception that marijuana is what they need to solve their problems causes constant abuse. Being without their stash and are constantly concerned with the next hit are hated by addicts. In a nutshell, you live, breathe and dream Marijuana. Some classic symptoms are:

Marijuana tolerance: the need for markedly in increased amounts of marijuana to achieve intoxication or markedly diminished effect with continued use of the same amount of Marijuana.

Greater use of marijuana than intended: Marijuana taken in larger amounts or over a longer period than was intended.

- ✓ To cut down or control marijuana use there are unsuccessful efforts.
- ✓ For using marijuana a great deal of time is spent.
- ✓ Marijuana use causing a reduction in social, occupational or recreational activities.
- ✓ significant problems will be caused due to continued use of marijuana despite knowing about it.

Marijuana and Addiction-Myths and Facts

There are several myths surrounding the use of Marijuana; however you should remember that interpretations vary - so the reader is urged to keep an open mind.

Cause for Permanent Mental Illness During intoxication, marijuana users become irrational and often behave erratically.

Even though there are not any scientific evidence showing that marijuana causes psychological damage or mental illness, psychological distress like feelings of panic, anxiety, and paranoia are caused following marijuana ingestion.

Marijuana is Highly Addictive. To break the addiction long term users experiencing physical dependence and withdrawal often need professional drug treatment.

It is not for those who smoke Marijuana occasionally and in very small quantities but for those who are long term users.

Being more potent than in the past. The youth of today are using a much more dangerous drug than their counterparts from the past ever did.

This is a highly debatable point as common sense tells us it must be true considering that man has always tried to improve everything so why not Marijuana.

Marijuana offences are not severely punished. Few marijuana addicts are arrested or sent to prison this encourages the continued use of the drug.

Statistics show this is far from the truth - arrests have more than doubled and keep increasing. They do get arrested, tried and jailed and make no mistake about that. The Law in every country in the world wishes to see the end of the drug rule - be it Marijuana or any other drug.

Causes more damage to lungs than tobacco. There is elevated risk of developing lung cancer and related diseases to marijuana smokers.

The belief that moderate marijuana smoking poses minimal danger to the lungs has been under dispute. No obstruction of the lung's small airway is exhibited by heavy marijuana smokers, unlike heavy tobacco smokers. No matter what it is you are smoking it has some effects so get wise.

Should Marijuana Be Legalized?

Legalizing any drug evokes strong emotions from people on both sides. This article is not intended to be an opinion piece, but rather an effort us look at some broad issues, facts, and monetary concerns regarding the potential legalization of marijuana.

In the United States, marijuana is currently classified as a Schedule 1 narcotic. That category indicates it has no medicinal use and a high abuse potential. There have been attempts over the past 2 decades to shift it into a different category, but unsuccessful. It is obvious there is lack of a consensus as to whether it has medicinal properties, as 15 states as of 2011 have legalized its usage for multiple medical conditions.

Is it reasonable for the US to continue classifying marijuana as such when other addictive and cancerous substances like nicotine are allowed? That is a hot button topic. The link between tobacco and various cancers is clear, yet it is big business and it does produce tax monies. There are clear labels on these products, yet over 20% of the American public smokes.

A 2002 Time magazine poll showed an amazing 80% of Americans supported legalizing medical marijuana. In the early 20th Century, artists and intellectuals were frequent users of marijuana for the purpose of enhancing creativity. By the mid

1920's, the American media had latched on to the idea that there was a connection between marijuana and crime, both violent and sexual. It is pretty clear at this point that is not true at all, but then even without any research to back up that fallacy all states had laws by the 1930's regulating marijuana usage.

The Commissioner of Narcotics at the time, Harry Anslinger, crusaded against marijuana in front of congress, the medical establishment, and the media warning against its dangers to society. As a result, in 1937, congressional hearings ensued with the result being the Marijuana Tax Act of 1937. This did not make marijuana illegal, but created a hefty tax structure around every part of the marijuana cycle (cultivation, distribution, sale). The onerous nature of the Act pushed marijuana usage to a negligible status.

Finally in the 1940's research began coming out showing marijuana to be relatively harmless compared to hard drugs like cocaine and heroin. The association with violence became negated and understood to be most likely from the alcohol being consumed in conjunction with marijuana. However, with the legal structure placed around grass the general public, saw it as dangerous despite a growing body of research showing it to be relatively (not completely) harmless.

During the 1950's and 60's marijuana use increased, but research mostly focused on LSD and other hard drugs. By 1970, the National Institute of Mental Health reported that 20 million Americans had used marijuana at least once. In 1970, a Gallup poll showed that 42% of college students had smoked marijuana.

As more and more research shows that marijuana does not contribute to violent behavior, it seems only natural that people would feel they've been lied to by the government agencies who are in charge of interpreting these issues. Marijuana has to be obtained illegally for medicinal usage in 35 states to this day, and patients have to live in fear of federal prosecution. Should marijuana law and policy be re-considered? Should it simply be re-considered for medicinal usage or for overall usage and be sold next to cigarettes, cigars, and alcohol?

In the 1970's, there was a push to de-criminalize small amounts of marijuana. For those supporting decriminalization, the general view was that the laws against marijuana were more harmful than the drug itself. President Jimmy Carter in 1977 called for the decriminalization of small amounts, so did the American Medical Association and American Bar Association. It didn't happen.

The 1980's saw a reverse of these efforts, and with President Reagan the War on Drugs ensued with tougher policies and penalties on pretty much every drug. Marijuana usage went down during this decade while alcohol, cocaine, and crack skyrocketed. The 1990's saw a reversal of usage trends. Between 1992 and 1994, marijuana usage doubled in adolescents.

Marijuana is not harmless. The cannabis plant has over 400 chemicals in it, and there's a lot we don't know about it. Should it be illegal though? Should it still be a Schedule 1 Narcotic? It is a big cash crop and regulating it could bring in significant tax monies along with eliminating the need to provide resources for so much prosecution. Many medical and scientific professionals have produced evidence about marijuana's medicinal benefits, and 15 states have allowed for its usage for debilitating conditions.

A recent study showed marijuana can have long lasting effects on adolescent brains, and it can affect coordination and mental capacity while under its effects. So this needs to be weighed in the pros vs cons debate. The "illegal" label promotes a significant negative aura in people's minds, and the robust debating has shown no evidence of letting up

WHAT ARE THE MEDICAL BENEFITS OF MARIJUANA?

Over the years, research has yielded results to suggest that marijuana may be of benefit in the treatment of some conditions. These are listed below.

Chronic pain

Last year, a large review from the National Academies of Sciences, Engineering, and Medicine assessed more than 10,000 scientific studies on the medical benefits and adverse effects of marijuana.

One area that the report looked closely at was the use of medical marijuana to treat chronic pain. Chronic pain is a leading cause of disability, affecting more than 25 million adults in the U.S.

The review found that marijuana, or products containing cannabinoids — which are the active ingredients in marijuana, or other compounds that act on the same receptors in the brain as marijuana are effective at relieving chronic pain.

Alcoholism and drug addiction

Another comprehensive review of evidence, published last year in the journal Clinical Psychology Review, revealed that using marijuana may help people with alcohol or opioid dependencies to fight their addictions.

But this finding may be contentious; the National Academies of Sciences review suggests that marijuana use actually drives increased risk for abusing, and becoming dependent on, other substances.

Also, the more that someone uses marijuana, the more likely they are to develop a problem with using marijuana. Individuals who began using the drug at a young age are also known to be at increased risk of developing a problem with marijuana use.

Depression, post-traumatic stress disorder, and social anxiety

The review published in Clinical Psychology Review assessed all published scientific literature that investigated the use of marijuana to treat symptoms of mental illness.

Evidence to date suggests that marijuana could help to treat some mental health conditions.

Its authors found some evidence supporting the use of marijuana to relieve depression and post-traumatic stress disorder symptoms.

That being said, they caution that marijuana is not an appropriate treatment for some other mental health conditions, such as bipolar disorder and psychosis.

The review indicates that there is some evidence to suggest that marijuana might alleviate symptoms of social anxiety, but again, this is contradicted by the National Academies of Sciences, Engineering, and Medicine review, which instead found that regular users of marijuana may actually be at increased risk of social anxiety.

Cancer

Evidence suggests that oral cannabinoids are effective against nausea and vomiting caused by chemotherapy, and some small studies have found that smoked marijuana may also help to alleviate these symptoms.

Some studies on cancer cells suggest that cannabinoids may either slow down the growth of or kill some types of cancer. However, early studies that tested this hypothesis in humans revealed that although cannabinoids are a safe treatment, they are not effective at controlling or curing cancer.

Multiple sclerosis

The short-term use of oral cannabinoids may improve symptoms of spasticity among people with multiple sclerosis, but the positive effects have been found to be modest.

Epilepsy

In June 2018, the Food and Drug Administration (FDA) approved the use of a medication containing cannabidiol (CBD) to treat two rare, severe, and specific types of epilepsy — called Lennox-Gastaut syndrome and Dravet syndrome that are difficult to control with other types of medication. This CBD-based drug is known as Epidiolex.

CBD is one of many substances that occurs in cannabis. It is not psychoactive. The drug for treating these conditions involves a purified form of CBD. The approval was based on the findings of research and clinical trials.

Dravet syndrome seizures are prolonged, repetitive, and potentially lethal. In fact, 1 in 5 children with Dravet syndrome do not reach the age of 20 years.

In the study, 120 children and teenagers with Dravet syndrome, all of whom were aged between 2 and 18, were randomly assigned to receive an oral CBD solution or a placebo for 14 weeks, along with their usual medication.

Research indicates that marijuana could help to treat epilepsy.

The researchers found that the children who received the CBD solution went from having around 12 seizures per month to an average of six seizures per month. Three children receiving CBD did not experience any seizures at all.

Children who received the placebo also saw a reduction in seizures, but this was slight their average number of seizures went down from 15 each month before the study to 14 seizures per month during the survey.

The researchers say that this 39 percent reduction in seizure occurrence provides strong evidence that the compound can help people living with Dravet syndrome, and that their paper has the first rigorous scientific data to demonstrate this.

However, the study also found a high rate of side effects linked to CBD. More than 9 in 10 of the children treated with CBD experienced side effects most commonly vomiting, fatigue, and fever.

The patient information leaflet for Epidiolex warns of side effects such as liver damage, sedation, and thoughts of suicide.

What are the health risks of marijuana?

At the other end of the spectrum is the plethora of studies that have found negative associations between marijuana use and health. They are listed below.

Mental health problems

Daily marijuana use is believed to exacerbate existing symptoms of bipolar disorder among people who have this mental health problem. However, the National Academies of Sciences, Engineering, and Medicine report suggests that among people with no history of the condition, there is only limited evidence of a link between marijuana use and developing bipolar disorder.

Moderate evidence suggests that regular marijuana users are more likely to experience suicidal thoughts, and there is a small increased risk of depression among marijuana users.

Marijuana use is likely to increase risk of psychosis, including schizophrenia. But a curious finding among people with schizophrenia and other psychoses is that a history of marijuana use is linked with improved performance on tests assessing learning and memory.

Testicular cancer

Although there is no evidence to suggest any link between using marijuana and an increased risk for most cancers, the National Academies of Sciences did find some evidence to suggest an increased risk for the slow-growing seminoma subtype of testicular cancer.

Respiratory disease

Regular marijuana smoking is linked to increased risk of chronic cough, but "it is unclear" whether smoking marijuana worsens lung function or increases the risk of chronic obstructive pulmonary disease or asthma.

A 2014 study that explored the relationship between marijuana use and lung disease suggested that it was plausible that smoking marijuana could contribute to lung cancer, though it has been difficult to conclusively link the two.

The authors of that study published in the journal Current Opinion in Pulmonary Medicine conclude:

"There is unequivocal evidence that habitual or regular marijuana smoking is not harmless. A caution against regular heavy marijuana usage is prudent."

"The medicinal use of marijuana is likely not harmful to lungs in low cumulative doses," they add, "but the dose limit needs to be defined. Recreational use is not the same as medicinal use and should be discouraged."

So, is marijuana good or bad for your health?

There is evidence that demonstrates both the harms and health benefits of marijuana. Yet despite the emergence over the past couple of years of very comprehensive, up-to-date reviews of the scientific studies evaluating the benefits and harms of the drug, it's clear that more research is needed to fully determine the public health implications of rising marijuana use.

More research is needed to confirm the harms and benefits of marijuana use.

Many scientists and health bodies including the American Cancer Society (ACS) support the need for further scientific research on the use of marijuana and cannabinoids to treat medical conditions.

However, there is an obstacle to this: marijuana is classed as a Schedule I controlled substance by the Drug Enforcement Administration, which deters the study of marijuana and cannabinoids through its imposition of strict conditions on the researchers working in this area.

If you happen to live in a state where medical use of marijuana is legal, you and your doctor will need to carefully consider these factors and how they relate to your illness and health history before using this drug.

For instance, while there is some evidence to support the use for marijuana for pain relief, you should certainly avoid marijuana if you have a history of mental health problems.

Remember to always speak to your doctor before taking a new medicine.

GROWING WEED FOR DUMMIES

You've probably fantasized what it would be like to have an entire field of weed all to yourself. Well, why not make the fantasy come true? Growing weed is, after all, kind of like the Holy Grail of the cannabis world. The 10 simple steps for growing weed below will walk you through the basics for growing your very own marijuana plant right at home.

1: Get Some Killer Seed

The right seed produces the right weed. There are a sh•t ton of strains and hybrids out there for you to mess around with, so as you become a more experienced grower try experimenting with different seeds.

To get you started, though, it's probably easiest to order from an online vendor. Browse their sites to see what sounds good to you and put in your order.

2: Find the Best Growing Container

As soon as your little package of marijuana seeds show up at your house, it's time to get those little ladies a home.

When it comes to picking out the right container for growing weed, start with something about the same size as a 5-gallon bucket and be sure it has plenty of drainage holes.

Go with either a deep gardening pot, a fabric pot, or a sturdy bucket with holes drilled into the bottom.

The critical thing here is that you don't want your plant sitting in a bunch of soggy, undrained soil—this could damage your plant's roots or lead to mold.

3: Use an Awesome Soil Mix

The easiest growing medium for beginning cannabis growers is a good, organic potting soil mix.

Look for soil that's got a good mixture of nutrients, things like coco fiber, compost, earthworm castings, bat guano, peat moss, and kelp meal.

But stay away from anything with "extended" or "slow release" nutrients since these additives can throw off the plant in its flowering stage.

4: Sprout the Cannabis Seed

All right, now that the prep work is done, it's time to plant that seed. Gently plant the seed 1/2-1 inch deep. Water it until the soil is thoroughly moist and put it in a warm place.

5: Water Your Baby Sprout

It's important to not let your baby sprout dry out. Keep it moist by gently watering it with a spray bottle. The first leaves your sprout will put out will be rounded and won't look like marijuana leaves. That's OK, it's the first step in your new baby's life. Give it some time, and soon it'll put out its first, tiny recognizable marijuana leaves.

6: Let There Be Light

By the time your baby has put out its first recognizable leaves, it's time to start focusing on light. In a lot of ways, light management is the most important aspect of cannabis cultivation, so try your to get your weed growing brain to focus here. You need to provide your little pot plant with at least 18 hours of light a day.

This means you'll most likely need to use a fluorescent lamp to be sure your plant gets all the light it needs.

As long as the plant gets 18 or more hours of light in a day, it will think it's in the "vegetation" phase, which means it will put all its energy into establishing roots and growing itself into a big, bushy, strong, and healthy plant.

It won't bud for a few more months, but if you're patient during the vegetation phase and you give it all the light, it wants. Your plant will reward you with some serious bud production later on.

7: Feed Your Plant

Throughout the cannabis plant's growing phase, you should feed it with some high-quality fertilizer. There are a bunch of things you can use to feed your little plant, but the simplest thing to do is get some plant food that's been specially formulated for the specific needs of cannabis plants.

You can also check out this page for a bunch of other ideas on what to feed your weed plant including wood ash, compost, vinegar and baking soda, even your piss.

8: Give Your Plant Some Loving

The vegetation phase is the longest and most important aspect of a cannabis plant's life, so be sure you're giving it some tender loving care while it's growing up.

Here are the keys:

- ✓ After you water the plant, wait until the top inch of soil is dry before watering it again.
- ✓ Be sure your plant is kept at a comfortable temperature: 70-85° F (20-30°C) is ideal.
- ✓ Keep an eye out for mold, spots, disease, or fungus and carefully remove any damaged leaves.
- ✓ Follow fertilizer directions to maintain healthy soil and encourage strong growth.
- ✓ Keep those lights on.

9: Trigger the Flowering Cycle

Growing Weed for Dummies: 10 Simple Steps to Get You Started

Once your plant has grown to the size you want it to, it's time to trigger the flowering cycle. You do this by cutting back on the amount of light it gets.

When you're ready to make your plant start to flower, it's time to start giving your plant a longer "night," somewhere around 12 hours of darkness a day should do the trick.

To keep it simple, stick with a 12/12 pattern to induce intense flowering—12 hours of light, 12 hours of dark.

10: Harvest, Dry, & Cure

At this point of the growing weed process, things are getting exciting. You're almost there, so stick with the directions just a little bit longer.

When your plant has produced its buds, it's time to harvest! Cut the buds away from the plant and remove any large stems or leaves.

Find somewhere where you can hang the buds to dry for a few days.

A few times a day, check how dry the buds are getting, and as soon as the smaller stems start snapping and only the thicker stems are bendable, it's time to move on to the curing stage.

To cure your weed, which experts will all tell you is key to getting the best flavor and the most potency out of your herb simply place all those dried buds into glass Mason jars and screw on the lids.

Keep the jars in a dark place and check their moisture content every once in a while. If it's too moist, let it air out a bit, until the buds are nice and perfectly sticky.

You've finished growing weed; now it's time to celebrate your harvest. Those little seeds you planted 4 months ago have now sprouted, grown, flowered, and it's time to sit back and enjoy the fruits of your labor. Light one up and get ready for your next round of planting.

TREATMENT CONSIDERATIONS FOR MARIJUANA ADDICTION

One of the easiest types of drug to obtain is marijuana. It's no wonder that marijuana addiction is becoming more and more common. While some people believe that marijuana isn't an addictive drug, the reality is that it is just as addictive as any other drug.

In fact, studies show that marijuana abusers exhibit the same, or similar symptoms as any other drug abuser. The fact is that many marijuana abusers simply cannot stop using, even when they wish to do so.

When marijuana addicts attempt to stop "smoking weed", they run into the same problems as other addicts. While it might be possible for the addict to stop using the drug for a short period of time there is nearly always a relapse unless the addict follows an established marijuana addiction treatment program protocol.

Unless the addict enrolls in a marijuana addiction treatment program, marijuana addiction cannot be treated effectively.

Symptoms Of Marijuana Dependence

Marijuana users exhibit the same symptoms as users of "heavy drugs." Among the most common is the psychological craving for the controlled substance when not using it.

The marijuana addict is haunted by constant thoughts of how to find more weed. This craving causes the addict to disregard legal constraints or even his own personal safety. When unable to obtain marijuana, the abuser will appear anxious or depressed.

Marijuana can cause some very severe negative conse□uences. Users routinely suffer some level of memory loss, anxiety and depression.

Withdrawal And Isolation

Even though marijuana is often labeled as a "social drug", these symptoms often compound the problem by causing the user to withdraw from society in favor of a life of isolation. These consequences not only affect the marijuana user, but also his or her family and friends.

Effects Of Smoking Weed On The Family

One of the reasons marijuana abuse needs to be taken seriously is that it negatively impacts the marijuana user's family, children and friends.

However, as family and friends begin to confront the user about his or her weed addiction, he or she usually withdraws further, thereby leading to a downward spiral into further isolation and depression.

Marijuana Addiction Is Not A Self Help Project

When it comes to marijuana dependency, the addict's problem is everyone's problem. It needs to be taken seriously. Ignoring the addict will not make the problem go away. Professional intervention is the only way to help the marijuana addict in the long term.

Fortunately, treatment for marijuana addiction is almost always successful as long as the patient, family and friends are all willing to work together with an established drug treatment center.

CONCLUSION

Evaluating the effects, addictiveness and their impacts, marijuana was rated as having a moderate impact on the consumers. Marijuana is made of dried, shredded leaves, stems, seeds, and flowers of the hemp plant (Cannabis Saliva). It can come in many different forms but the most common one is the dried leaves and its appearance is long green leaves.

The short term affects are not great (drowsiness, lack of motor control and decreased level of energy) and they only last for a short amount of time (about two hours after the drug is ingested). Unfortunately, if marijuana is taken frequently long term effects begin to appear, they are more severe and they can last a lifetime. Long term, marijuana smoked (the most common method of entrance to the bloodstream) can completely destroy the respiratory system, leading to the individual developing a chronic cough vastly increasing the risk of heart failures and cancer. Marijuana smoke has a higher amount of cancer producing agents than tobacco smoke. Marijuana can also cause brain damage if taken regularly.

Some symptoms include memory loss, short attention span and perpetual drowsiness leading to loss of jobs and educational failures. Marijuana is not very addictively (only 9% of users are addicted but that doesn't seem to stop people taking it. Studies show that in 2010 of the estimated 7.1 million Americans classified with dependence on or abuse of illicit drugs, nearly 4.5 million were dependent on or abused marijuana. The withdrawal symptoms of the drug has a moderate impact such as higher craving and sleeplessness. The marijuana consumers have said that they would and could withdraw from the drug any day and the effects are not as strong. If marijuana users were educated on the negative effects of marijuana, they might be compelled to stop using it.

Overall, the impact of the drug is moderate and it can affect the consumers in many ways but they are not extreme. Marijuana exhibits a mix of all properties including stimulants, depressants and hallucinogens so it can work for any type of pain someone experiences. Because the short term symptoms are not great, marijuana can be used as a medicine, but it is unwise to do so for long periods of time and without a doctor's recommendation.

Therefore, for the reasons described above it is believed that

Marijuana should be rated as a two.

Do Not Go Yet; One Last Thing To Do

If you enjoyed this book or found it useful, I'd be very grateful if

you'd post a short review on Amazon. Your support does make a

difference, and I read all the reviews personally so I can get your

feedback and make this book even better.

Thanks again for your support!